CREEPY, KOOKY SCIENCE

Killer Carnivorous Plants

Nathan Aaseng

Enslow Publishing
101 W. 23rd Street
Suite 240
New York, NY 10011
USA
enslow.com

Published in 2019 by Enslow Publishing, LLC.
101 W. 23rd Street, Suite 240, New York, NY 10011

Copyright © 2019 by Nathan Aaseng

All rights reserved.

No part of this book may be reproduced by any means without the written permission of the publisher.

Library of Congress Cataloging-in-Publication Data
Names: Aaseng, Nathan, author.
Title: Killer carnivorous plants / Nathan Aaseng.
Description: New York : Enslow Publishing, 2019. | Series: Creepy, kooky science | Audience: Grade 5-8. | Includes bibliographical references and index.
Identifiers: LCCN 2018014736| ISBN 9781978504509 (library bound) | ISBN 9781978505513 (paperback)
Subjects: LCSH: Carnivorous plants—Juvenile literature.
Classification: LCC QK917 .A2 2019 | DDC 583/.887—dc23
LC record available at https://lccn.loc.gov/2018014736

Printed in the United States of America

To Our Readers: We have done our best to make sure all websites in this book were active and appropriate when we went to press. However, the author and the publisher have no control over and assume no liability for the material available on those websites or on any websites they may link to. Any comments or suggestions can be sent by email to customerservice@enslow.com.

Portions of this book originally appeared in *Weird Meat-Eating Plants*.

Photo Credits: Cover, p. 1 Dejawu/Shutterstock.com; p. 6 AF archive/Alamy Stock Photo; p. 8 Chirasak Tolertmongkol/Shutterstock.com; p. 12 Scenics & Science/Alamy Stock Photo; p. 15 Jojoo64/Shutterstock.com; p. 17 annick de caluwe1980/Shutterstock.com; p. 20 Paul Starosta/Corbis Documentary/Getty Images; p. 22 Quinn Aikens/Shutterstock.com; p. 25 mccw thissen/Shutterstock.com; p. 26 Sanevich/Shutterstock.com; p. 29 Marco Uliana/Shutterstock.com; p. 32 Luka Hercigonja/Shutterstock.com; p. 34 Kim Taylor/Nature Picture Library/Getty Images; p. 37 nico99/Shutterstock.com; p. 38 Chloe Langton/Shutterstock.com; p. 41 By Chun photographer/Shutterstock.com.

CHAPTER 1

Discovering Killer Plants

In 1760, English settlers along the North Carolina coast discovered a plant that came to be known as the Venus flytrap. They watched in fascination as this plant snapped shut when insects landed on it, and squeezed the insects to death.

Are They Killers or Not?

This triggered a great debate among scientists. Could this plant be trapping and eating these insects? Some believed the plant actually was carnivorous. But many said no, and thought the trap was just another ingenious way for the plant to protect itself against pests. Even the world's foremost botanist, Carolus Linneaus (1707–1778) of Sweden, refused to believe that the plant intentionally killed insects and other creatures for food. Such a thing, he

These are pitcher plants known as monkey cups. Pitcher plants filled with insects floating in water led to questions. Were these accidental deaths, or were plants purposely trapping them?

believed, was not possible because it went against nature.[1] Plants do not have mouths or stomachs for digesting meals. How could they possibly eat animals?

Meanwhile, for many years, people had noticed pools of water inside of the pitcher plants that grew in North American and the Pacific tropics. Often, they discovered dead and decomposing insects floating in that liquid. Were these dead bugs the result of accidents, or was the plant intentionally killing them?

In 1857, researcher Ferdinand Cohn (1828–1898) examined one of the tiny sacs on an aquatic plant called a bladderwort. Most people who knew of these sacs thought that they served as buoys to keep the plant afloat. But when the scientist opened one up, he discovered a tiny dead fish. He then placed some water fleas in an aquarium filled with bladderworts. Before long the bladderwort sacks were filled with the fleas.[2] About twenty years later, naturalist Mary Treat (1830–1923) found that the sac was a trap that could engulf tiny water creatures in the blink of an eye.

Arguments over whether plants were doing the unimaginable by devouring small animals continued. This debate reached a fever pitch when scientists discovered a partially digested rat inside a large pitcher plant. Was this another accident, or were there plants that actually ate animals the size of a rat?

No Accident

The famed English biologist Charles Darwin (1809–1882) was among many

Is It a Carnivorous Plant?

Since Darwin's time, botanists have identified more than 670 species of carnivorous plants. According to the Carnivorous Plant Society, these three criteria must be met in order to be considered a carnivorous plant:

1. "The plant must have clear adaptations to capture prey, such as a trap."
2. "The plant must have some way to digest the prey into a form that can be absorbed by the plant."
3. "The plant must have some way of absorbing the nutrients, and must benefit from the nutrients."[3]

who set out to answer the question once and for all. In 1875, he reported the results of a long series of experiments in which he first proved that the trapping of insect in these plants was no accident. The plants did not trap just anything that landed on them. They only worked when certain nutrients, available in insects, were present.

Darwin then showed that these plants produced digestive juices that contained enzymes, much like the digestive enzyme found in animals. His careful measurements, documented in a 275-page report showed that after the insects were killed, these nutrients were absorbed by the plant. Furthermore, his experiments showed that carnivorous plants were gaining nutrition from their meals. Plants that were fed an occasional meaty meal proved to be healthier than those given no meat.[4]

Carnivorous plants live in many types of climates from the arctic to the tropics. Most live in places with wet, spongey soil, called bogs. As many as thirteen species have been discovered in a single bog.[5] But a few species can be found in deserts and mountains. What their habitats all have in common is that they tend to be lacking in nutrients such as nitrogen, phosphorus, and sulfur. Because they are able to obtain these nutrients from animals, carnivorous plants are able to thrive in such places.

Most carnivorous plants are fairly small. Their prey is mostly tiny, such as insects, spiders, and tiny water creatures. However, there are plants capable of devouring animals as large as rats, mice, lemurs, frogs, snakes, and small birds. Others dine on scorpions, spiders, grasshoppers, wasps, flies, ants, slugs, snails, baby fish, and tadpoles.

Tiny Killers

Even the small plant carnivores are no less fascinating for their size. Some of the tiniest animals in our world must indeed tread carefully or else they will become meals for plants. Beware the killer grasses! *Molinia caerulea,* for example, is a grass that catches and eats insects for a brief time in its life. The grass has small traps on it that spring shut on small prey.

Beware the killer fungi! Fungi are in a different biological kingdom than plants, but as many as two hundred different kinds of fungi attack from the ground just like plants.[6] One fungus, called *Arthrobotrys obligiospora,* contains looped structures. The loop draws tight as tiny creatures, such as eelworms, crawl through it. The fungus then digests its victim. Another fungus, *Zoophagus insidians,* sets a trap for tiny animals called rotatoria. It sends out short branches for the rotatoria to feed on. As the rotatorium takes a bite, the tip of the branch swells, and the feeder is trapped.

Some small animals must even beware of killer seeds! Seeds of a plant known as *Capsella bursa-pastoris*, or shepherd's purse, use a very pleasant chemical aroma to attract mosquito larvae.

Seeds from the *Capsella bursa-pastoris*, shown here in the pod, kill insect larvae and absorb the nutrients.

When the larvae arrive, the seeds release a poison that kills them. The seeds then release an enzyme to digest the prey so that it can be absorbed.

With the exception of a few species that display wicked-looking fangs or a low row of sharp curved hooks, most carnivorous plants appear harmless. The do not have the intimidating presence of carnivores such as tigers or wolves. They tend to look peaceful, even inviting. The carnivorous plants are among the most beautiful in nature, with delicate flowers of yellow, purple, and white. Their leaves may be etched with graceful designs of green, purple, red, and pink.

Hidden within this quiet beauty, however, are deadly traps that make these plants as effective at capturing prey as the most feared hunters in the world.

CHAPTER 2

Sticky Traps

Many common plants such as the petunia have a sticky substance on their leaves that acts like flypaper to trap and kill tiny insects. But these are strictly defensive measures to protect the plant from pests. Carnivorous plants have found a way to lure prey onto a surface filled with a substance so sticky that escape is impossible. Then they devour their prey.

Butterworts: Innocent-Looking Killers

There are seventy-nine species of *Pinguicula*, or butterworts, that live in most parts of the world north of the equator.[1] Butterworts are plants that blend easily into the background. Nothing about them suggests their killer nature. Their yellow-green leaves lie flat to the ground in a circle pattern called a rosette. These leaves appear to be greasy rather than sticky. In fact, their name comes

There is nothing in the plain appearance of a common butterwort to warn of the danger that awaits tiny creatures.

from the buttery feel of the leaves. Generally, only the tiniest, lightest insects need fear getting trapped in this coating.

Their most common prey, the gnat, is attracted by the plant's musty aroma. It flies closer to locate the source of this attractive smell and lands on one of its leaves. Too late, the unlucky insect discovers that the aroma was a lure. Its legs are now stuck in the greasy substance. The gnat struggles to get free. As it does, the plant produces more of the greasy substance. Before long, the thrashing gnat is so coated with the substance that it suffocates to death.

The butterwort then releases enzymes to digest the nutrients in the insect. Slowly, the leaf curls slightly to form a shallow saucer, which keeps the enzymes from spilling out. The butterwort also bathes the dead gnat in an antibiotic. This kills bacteria feeding on the prey that would otherwise consume nutrients and could spread and cause harm to the plant.[2] The antibiotic is so effective, it was used by humans in treating wounds long before the plant was known to be carnivorous.

Butterworts are not fussy eaters. The butterwort's leaves will curl up and digest anything, including seeds and bits of plant material containing nitrogen, which is present in all living things.

Sundews: Sparkling Killers

The 152 species of *Drosera*, or sundews, are somewhat more lively flypaper killers. Rather than waiting for the prey to suffocate itself, the sundews work to make the job go faster.

A British scientist once wandered across a killing field that clearly showed both the carnivorous plants' incredible beauty and their deadly menace to small creatures. A dense carpet of low-growing sundew plants spread for nearly two acres in a remote, spongy bog. Droplets of clear liquid sparkled like diamonds on each plant.

A huge cloud of migrating butterflies swarmed to the meadow for a rest before they continued their journey. They never left. The butterflies stuck to the little jeweled droplets and could not escape. As many as seven butterflies writhed in their death throes on a single plant. The scientist estimated that this sundew stand killed six million butterflies in a single afternoon![3]

Sundews are the largest group of meat-eating plants. They can be found in climates as diverse as Australia and Alaska.[4]

A sundew glistens with drops of a sticky substance that can trap unsuspecting visitors.

Facebook Helps Science

Social media has had an effect on scientific research on sundews. The *Drosera magnifica* was first called to botanists' attention by Facebook pictures posted by tourists visiting a mountain in southeastern Brazil. Intrigued by this, a group of scientists went to investigate. Thus, they discovered the largest sundew ever found in the Americas, a plant with stems up to 5 feet (1.8 meters) long. This species of sundew has never been found anywhere else but on that mountaintop.[5]

Some are no larger than a penny, while other varieties grow as large as a small bush.

Sundews are strikingly beautiful, especially when their beads of nectar, which look like morning dew, glisten in the sun. These beads rest on top of tentacles, which are thin, reddish, hair-like stalks that rise up from the sundew's flat leaves.

A butterfly or gnat fluttering over a field detects the sparkle and sweet nectar of a sundew and stops to take a sample. As soon as it lands, it finds that the nectar is combined with a sticky substance called mucilage. The insect's wings or legs get caught. Its attempts to pull away from the mucilage trigger the plant's lethal response.

The plant has a unique way of telling a meal from a piece of dirt or a raindrop. Although these things may be heavier than the insects that land on it, the plant will not waste time and energy on them. Only when it feels movement will it prepare for the kill.

Unlike animals, plants have no central nervous system to coordinate their movement. Yet somehow each tentacle on the leaf gets the message to bend in the direction of the prey to get as many glands as possible in contact with the victim.

The harder the prey struggles to free itself from the mucilage, the faster the tentacles move and the more mucilage pours out of the leaf. These tentacles aid digestion by holding the prey in the fluid. Some have leaves that fold around the prey for the same purpose. The sundew then releases acids and enzymes to digest the victim.

The prey suffers a most unpleasant death. It suffocates in the sticky fluid while being burned by acids and while its bodily fluids are being squeezed out. Some victims may struggle for hours. A few sundews have such powerful digestive systems that they can absorb a prey's nutrients in a matter of hours.

When the sundew is finished with the prey, the tentacles relax their grip and the leaf unfurls. It takes from one to three days for the leaf surface to dry so that the plant can prepare for a new victim.

Sundews are not a danger to every insect that lands on them. The caterpillar of the plumed moth often feeds on the nectar of the plant without suffering any harm. But sundews can be deadly killers of insects. Botanists commonly find sundew leaves that are black with the bodies of the gnats it has killed.[6]

A single purple flower decorates a thorny-looking death trap known as a *Byblis liniflora*.

Byblis: Fatal Beauties

The *Byblis* are a much less common form of flypaper killer. These beautiful purple-flowered plants grow only in Australia. One species reaches a height of more than 2 feet (61 centimeters) and can intertwine with other *Byblis* plants to form a woody hedge. Although these plants tend to feed on small insects, it has been reported that large insects such as grasshoppers appear to be paralyzed by some chemical given off by the plant.[7] This curiosity is under further investigation.

CHAPTER 3

Pits of Death

While slogging through the bogs of Northern California and southern Oregon, you may come across a field of sinister-looking plants called *Darlingtonia,* the cobra lily. With its straight stalk topped by a rounded, spotted hood, this pitcher plant looks like a cobra poised to strike. As if that were not frightening enough, the cobra lily also displays two long, narrow projections that look like the fangs of a snake. They are not at all dangerous to humans, but they do mean death to a wide variety of insects.

You could also tramp through a bog along Alabama's Gulf Coast or in Minnesota's northern wetlands, and come across a field carpeted with *Sarracenia* pitcher plants. Row upon row of these beautiful plants with green and purple trumpet-shaped leaves and dangling yellow flowers spread before you. The scene

The *Darlingtonia* pitcher plant, also called the cobra lily, resembles the deadly snake for which it is named.

looks peaceful and innocent. This appearance, however, is misleading. These plants are as deadly as their close relative, the cobra lily. Once you know the fiendishly clever lengths these plants go to snare their victims, you can almost begin to hear that eerie music they play in scary movie scenes.

An Elaborate Trap

Pitcher plants have developed a more complex method of capturing meals than that of the flypaper trappers. Like the sundews and butterworts, they do not actively subdue their prey. But they present such a well-designed pitfall trap that the victim cannot resist walking straight into it to its death.

Pitcher plants are common in North America, especially in low-lying, damp, sandy areas. The pitchers are long leaves that rise from an underground stem called a rhizome. They form a hollow, vase-like tube that is wide at the top and narrows as it descend to the bottom of the plant. Part of the leaf may form a hood over the opening.

A pitcher plant is loaded with lures. Its bright, graceful leaves and sweet aroma entice prey. The hood provides shelter for insects and other small creatures who want to escape the rain. The undersurface of the hood contains glands that produce a sugary treat that insects enjoy. Some pitcher plants lay a trail of nectar that starts at ground level and leads up to the mouth of the pitcher. One kind of pitcher surrounds its hood with a white band coated with nectar that termites cannot resist.[1]

Once the prey lands on the hood, the pitcher plant lures it farther into the pitcher with more nectar. The hood and parts of the neck of the pitcher often lack color and may be nearly transparent. This allows light to shine down into the pitcher, so that insects are not afraid to go into it.

As the insect moves toward the mouth, it may slip on the smooth, waxy surface into a region lined with stiff hairs. Some prey try to reach over the hairs to get at the rich pool of nectar on the other side, but the nectar is just out of reach so that the insect will have to stretch far, and possibly fall down into the pitcher.

Point of No Return

After a time, a flying insect may try to get out while the getting is good. The hood lets in so much light that that it appears to be an opening to the outside. The insect that tries to fly through these fake windows smashes into the hood and falls back down into the pitcher.[2]

Some pitcher plants deaden their victim's senses with poisons. *Sarracenia flava*, for example, produces a substance that acts as a narcotic. As the insect laps up the nectar, it becomes less wary and less steady on its feet.[3]

Once an insect starts walking among the hairs, its fate is sealed. All the hairs point downward into the pitcher. While the insect can move around the hairs as it walks into the pitcher, it finds its way blocked by these hairs when it tries to turn around.

Just past the hairs, the surface of the pitcher plant becomes smooth and waxy. When the prey reaches this point, it has no hope of escape. Unable to get a grip with its feet, it slides further down into the pitcher until it falls into the pool of liquid at the bottom.

The pitcher plant seems to have thought of everything in laying this trap. Some pitchers contain toxins that stun the prey. Others have a wetting agent that soaks the wings of flying insects so they cannot fly out. The wetting agent also breaks the surface tension, which is the force that binds water molecules together and makes it possible for many insects to crawl on the surface of water. With the surface tension destroyed, the insects drown.

Meanwhile, enzymes trickle down the inside walls of the pitcher and collect in the bottom. Gradually, the plant digests the nutrients of the victim and absorbs them through special glands.

Like all pitcher plants, the *Sarracenia flava* lures insect visitors into a chamber from which there is no escape.

The rare *Nepenthes rajah* comes closest to the man-eating plants of legend. It grows large enough to occasionally trap animals such as frogs, rats, and lemurs.

Not all pitcher plants produce enzymes. The purple pitcher plant in Canada has to rely on help to digest its prey. Mosquito larvae living in the pool chew up the prey.[4]

After a time, the pool at the bottom may become filled with corpses of the plant's victims. Some plants have become so heavy with the weight of their dead prey that their stem cannot support the pitcher and they topple over.

Heavy rains can sometimes cause problems. Although the hood of the pitcher often keeps rain out, it is not always effective. One species of pitcher, known as the sun pitcher, lives high above the rain forest of South America where rain is almost constant. This plant has a hole in its base that drains water to keep the fluid in the bottom of the plant at the right level.[5]

Pitcher plants most commonly eat ants, flies, and beetles. They will also capture and devour crickets, wasps, spiders, and even small toads.

Giant Flesh Eaters

The *Nepenthes,* found in tropical regions of Asia, are different from most pitcher plants in that they grow like vines. They can creep along the soil or climb up tree trunks. These plants have long leaves that taper to a point and then form pitchers. The pitchers on the upper end of the vine are small and trumpet-shaped. Large, wide vases grow on the lower end.

Of all carnivorous plants, the *Nepenthes rajah* comes closest to the human-eating monsters of science fiction. This plant has gourd-like pitchers that may be 14 inches (36 cm) long and 6 inches (15 centimeters) in diameter and may hold as much as a gallon (about 4 liters) of water. Their gaping mouths have an ominous, blood-red color. These plants are extremely rare. Botanists estimate that there may be as few as two thousand *Nepenthes rajahs* in existence.[6]

These giant *Nepenthes* usually dine on cockroaches, centipedes, and scorpions as well as smaller insects. But larger animals, such as field mice, rats, small birds, frogs, and lemurs have been found dead in the bottoms of *Nepenthes*. The plants do not depend on these large victims, which are hard to digest, for food.

Feces as Food

Recently it has been found that shrews and bats have made life easier for some giant *Nepenthes*. They use the huge pitchers as a toilet and their waste products provide the plant with an easily absorbed form of nutrients that make predation virtually unnecessary.[7]

CHAPTER 4

Active Trigger Traps

One of the biggest differences between plants and animals is that animals have the ability to move, often quickly, while plants remain in one spot. The plants that act the most like animal predators are the ones with trigger traps that can strike in a blink of an eye. Unlike the flypapers and pitchers, which lure prey to a lethal spot and slowly kill them, trigger traps strike suddenly. Like the fierce predators of the animal world, they have something that works like a mouth to snap shut on their prey.

Darwin's "Wonderful Plant"

A trigger trap called *Dionaea*, or the Venus flytrap, is found only along the coastal plains of North and South Carolina. It was unknown to most of the world until two hundred years ago. When

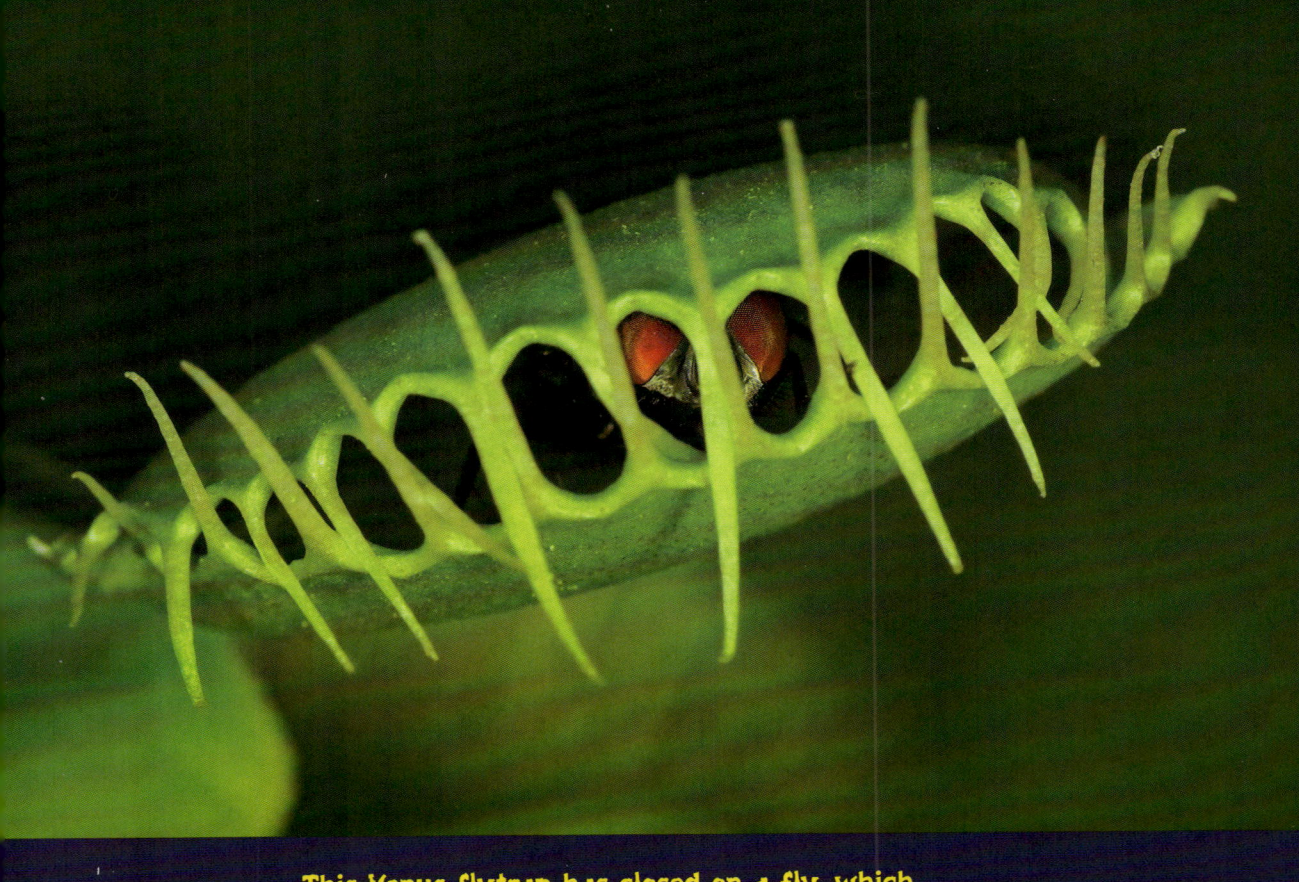

This Venus flytrap has closed on a fly, which cannot escape and now awaits digestion.

it was called to Charles Darwin's attention, he declared it one of the most wonderful plants in the world.[1] Among the plant's more amazing features is the fact that its trap serves as a mouth, stomach, and intestines all in one.[2]

The Venus flytrap's relatively large size and fascinating explosive action has made it the most famous of all carnivorous plants. This white-flowered plant usually contains a half dozen traps that may be as large as 3 inches (8 cm) across. The traps are leaves, divided into two lobes that look like a partially open clamshell.

Spines line the edges of these lobes. Three trigger hairs are arranged in a triangular pattern inside the trap.

The inside of the trap is bright red. Along with the usual sugary nectar, the color helps to lure an insect close to the trigger hairs. Because the flytrap does not want to waste time and energy on something it cannot use, the trap is triggered by motion. Even a dead insect or piece of meat laid in the trap will get no reaction.

As an insect feeds on the nectar, it brushes a trigger hair. This sends an electronic message to the rest of the leaf: prepare for action! Now the prey is one touch away from doom.

The plant has two ways of ensuring that whatever trigged the trap is worth eating. First, the nectar is placed far enough from the trigger hairs that a small feeding insect will not reach it. Second, this amazing plant can count! The trap will not shut unless two different hairs are touched or one hair is touched twice within twenty seconds. This prevents the trap from closing on a piece of debris that gets blown into it.[3]

When the trap is triggered, water rushes out of the inner cells of the leaf. This causes the two lobes to snap together in a fraction of a second.

The plant does not clamp completely shut at first. It closes just far enough for the spines to overlap, like iron bars on a jail cell. Again, the plant does this so as not to waste effort on small prey. The spines hold larger insects in, while smaller insects can scoot out between them. If no insect remains in the trap, it reopens within twenty-four hours.

If a suitable prey remains, the trap closes tightly. The two lobes squeeze together crushing soft-bodied insects and sealing the trap so that it turns into a digestive vat. The plant releases fluids that drown and digest the prey. The plant absorbs the nutrients, using a process that may take several days. Then it reopens, exposing the undigested remains, which fall off or blow away. The Venus flytrap is then ready for another victim.

The Venus flytrap's name is misleading. Generally, large ants and spiders each make up about one-third of its diet, with beetles and grasshoppers accounting for 10 percent each. Flies seldom provide more than 5 percent of the diet.[4]

But it eats whatever it catches, as long as the prey is the right size. This includes flies, spiders, snails, slugs, and tiny frogs.

Lightning Fast Attacks

The plants that are most deadly to tiny aquatic creatures are the *Utricularia,* or bladderworts. They use one of the most intricate mechanisms in the plant kingdom to snatch unsuspecting prey out of the water faster than the eye can see.

The 220 species of bladderworts are the most widespread of all plant carnivores, thriving from the arctic to the tropics. They are rootless plants that float free in shallow lakes, ponds, and quiet

The flowers of the bladderwort provide a misleading sense of delicate beauty on the surface, while its deadly traps below wait for victims to draw near.

streams, or anchor themselves loosely in water-soaked ground.

The majority of bladderworts actually live on land. Only about 20 percent of them are aquatic. The terrestrial ones are very difficult to see if they are not flowering, as they have small, plain leaves that hug the ground in wet soil. They catch microscopic worms and insects that dwell in the water below the soil.

Aquatic plants usually gulp only tiny invertebrates (animals without backbones), such as water mites, water fleas, and mosquito larvae.

The more common aquatic forms drift along the water, sending beautiful yellow or purple flowers above the surface. The business end of the plant lies below the surface. The bladderwort sends out a network of hair-like stems up to 10 feet (3 meters) in length. These stems are loaded with tiny balloon-like structures called bladders from which the plants get their name.

These bladders rarely grow as large as a quarter of an inch (0.6 cm) long. At one end of each bladder, there is a trapdoor that swings inward. Most of the time, this door is sealed shut by a sticky substance.

The bladderwort sets the trap by pumping some of the water out of its bladder. This helps create a partial vacuum inside the bladder. You can get the same effect by squeezing the rubber tip of an eyedropper. As soon as you release the tip, it sucks in liquid. The bladderwort's door, however, blocks water from coming into the bladder. The pressure remains, so the bladder is ready to suck in water as soon as the door opens.

Along comes a water creature so tiny that you would need a magnifying glass to see it. The creature begins to feed on what appear to be strands of algae. In fact, these strands are trigger hairs that surround the door opening.

Reset and Repeat

Bladderworts can trap a tremendous number of prey in a short time. But because their sac openings are so small, it would be difficult to notice bladders' kills even when the traps are snapping left and right. Occasionally, however, the force of the trap opening snares something larger, such as a newborn fish or a tadpole. Sometimes these unfortunate creatures are found with their heads stuck in bladderwort traps. A bladderwort can ingest one of these creatures by resetting the trap with the victim's head stuck inside and respringing the trap to suck in more. The traps can be reset within fifteen to thirty minutes.[5]

This mosquito larva's body, with its large head still sticking out, has been sucked into the bladderwort's sac.

When the creature touches one of these hairs, the door flies open with lightning speed. Water rushes into the trap with incredible power—six hundred times the force of gravity. The water sweeps the prey in with it. As soon as the water fills the bladder, the door closes. The entire process may take as little as one five-hundredth of a second. No creature on earth is fast enough to escape a trap that springs that quickly![6]

CHAPTER 5

Carnivorous Plants' Survival Manual

Ever since carnivorous plants were discovered, scientists have searched for answers to why they exist. How did plants develop a taste for meat? And how did they manage to defy the normal rules of nature to become predators of animals?

The answer is actually very simple: survival. All living things compete with other living things for food, water, and space. Any advantage that helps a species better compete for resources gives it a better chance for survival. Carnivorous plants have found this advantage in eating meat. Unlike animal meat-eaters, however, it is not the protein in their victims that helps them survive.

Surviving a Poor Environment

Most plants get the nutrients they need to survive, such as nitrogen, phosphorus, and sulfur, from the soil. Carnivorous plants commonly grow in soil that is a poor source of these nutrients.

If a plant had a way get these elements from someplace other than the soil, it would have an advantage over other plants in these environments. Carnivorous plants have done just that; they have gained this advantage by capturing insects and other small creatures that contain those scarce nutrients they need.

The advantage they gain from this is not large. Carnivorous plants do not need to eat creatures in order to live and grow. But actively trapping plants are more likely to be larger and healthier than plants that are not trapping in those areas. This gives them a better chance of survival.

How Did They Develop Such Amazing Traps?

No one knows for sure. But creature-trapping likely came about by accident. Many plants, not just carnivorous ones, are able to absorb nutrients through their leaves as well as roots. Some plants developed leaves that curled into shallow bowls. Water could have collected on these leaves in shallow pools that attracted insects. Some of these visitors could have accidentally drowned. The plants then absorbed nutrients from the dead insects, which gave them a survival advantage in areas with poor

Like all carnivorous plants, Venus flytraps make up for the poor quality of the soil by ingesting nutrients from their prey.

soil. Over millions of years, the plants developed leaves that were more and more helpful at capturing small creatures.[1]

People have long been fascinated with the idea of huge meat-eating plants capable of swallowing human beings. Could such creatures have existed, just as enormous dinosaurs once roamed the earth? The slim survival margin that carnivorous plants gain from their activities helps answer the question of why there are no giant people-eating plants.

Meat-eating provides plants only a small advantage in gaining nutrients. The advantage is worth the energy that the plant has to

Protected by a special substance that prevents it from sticking to adhesives, this caspid can roam at will among the deadliest of flypaper traps.

expend to capture and digest small creatures. A plant would need to use a huge amount of energy to capture and digest large animals. Bladderworts have great difficulty digesting the larger organisms that they catch. They may even die in the attempt. Venus flytraps turn black and die if they happen to catch a prey that is larger than what they normally can handle.[2]

Living with Their Neighbors

The fact that they have gained a competitive advantage does not mean that it is always easy for carnivorous plants to catch prey. Just as these plants have adapted ways to compete more efficiently, other creatures have adapted ways to beat these green carnivores's tricks. A wingless insect called a caspid, for example, has developed an antidote to the sticky glue of flypaper traps. It fearlessly walks up and down leaves that mean instant death to most other insects.

Hooded pitcher plants offer shade, warmth, shelter from rain, and a ready supply of food for any creature that can avoid their deadly traps. Many insects have accepted the challenge of living dangerously. At least sixteen species of insects are found nowhere else but inside pitcher plants![3]

Mosquito larvae and fly maggots wriggle among the carcasses in the pitcher's pool. Coated with a special substance that helps protect them from the plant's digestive enzymes, they feed on the rotting and half-digested remains of trapped prey.

One species of moth spins a net across the opening of the pitcher plant to form a roofed home. Protected from rain and other insects, these moths chew on the walls of the pitcher. They have no trouble crawling up and down the walls that are so deadly to most other insects. Their special claws allow them to cling to the downward-pointing hairs. They walk down the plant backward so they do not have to try to turn themselves around when they are wedged in by the hairs.

One kind of spider avoids the slippery walls of the pitcher altogether by spinning a silken lifeline on which it drops down to the bottom of the pitcher to collect meals captured by the plant.

The most deadly enemies of carnivorous plants are humans. People do not see much value in the boggy areas in which carnivorous plants thrive. Because of this, the natural homes of the carnivorous plants are dwindling quickly. Every year, millions of acres of these wetlands are drained, plowed under, turned into pasture or farm ponds, covered by housing or industrial developments, or paved over.

Growing Killer Plants at Home

The fact that carnivorous plants are such fascinating, exotic plants has resulted in people picking these plants just for the novelty of owning them. But there is no reason for anyone to pick any carnivorous plants in the wild. Many of them, including the Venus flytrap, are easy to grow in one's own home. The plants can be obtained from places that grow them from seeds or tissue. There are national and international organizations, along with books and websites, that provide information and advice about growing these amazing plants.

Carnivorous plants have also suffered from their own beauty. Their bright flowers and the striking network of green, purple, red, and pink veins in their leaves have made them an attractive part of floral arrangements. Millions of plants are picked for bouquets every year.

Nearly half of all species of carnivorous plants are listed as threatened, most through human activity. Because of habitat loss and over collection, even the popular Venus flytrap is listed as "vulnerable" by the Natural Wildlife Federation.[4] Botanists estimate that there are only thirty-three thousand of them still living in the wild, all of them within 75 miles (121 kilometers) of Wilmington, North Carolina. Concern over the fate of this incredible plant is so high that in 2014, the North Caroline legislature passed a law that makes picking a wild Venus flytrap a felony that could result in two years in prison.[5]

The beauty of carnivorous plants, as well their intriguing eating habits, make them a popular choice among gardeners.

Great care must be taken to ensure that the carnivorous plant species survive. Otherwise, the world could lose forever a fascinating group of plants—the curious little monster plants that have turned the tables on the animal world.

Chapter Notes

Introduction

1. Ron Sullivan and Joe Eaton, "The Dirt: Myths About Man-Eating Plants—Something to Chew On," *San Francisco Chronicle*, October 27, 2007, http://www.sfgate.com;homegardenarticle.
2. Randall Schwartz, *Carnivorous Plants* (New York, N.Y.: Praeger, 1974), pp. 122–123.

Chapter 1. Discovering Killer Plants

1. *Plants Behaving Badly*, directed by Steve Nicholls (Vienna, Austria: Terra Factual Studios, 2013), documentary.
2. Peter D'Amato, *The Savage Garden* (Berkeley, Calif.: Ten Speed Press, 2013), p. 270.
3. Barry Rice, "Frequently Asked Questions," International Carnivorous Plant Society, revised July 2011, http://www.sarracenia.com/faq/faq1040.html.
4. *Plants Behaving Badly*.
5. "Carnivorous Plants/Insectivorous Plants," Botanical Society of America, accessed April 30, 2018, https://botany.org/Carnivorous_Plants/.
6. David Malloch, "Fungal Parasites of Animals," Natural History of Fungi, New Brunswick Museum, accessed April 30, 2018, http://

website.nbm-mnb.ca/mycologywebpages/NaturalHistoryOfFungi/AnimalParasites.html.

Chapter 2. Sticky Traps

1. "Carnivorous Plants/Insectivorous Plants," Botanical Society of America, accessed April 30, 2018, https://botany.org/Carnivorous_Plants/.
2. Peter D'Amato, *The Savage Garden* (Berkeley, Calif.: Ten Speed Press 2013), p. 237.
3. Michael Lipski, "Forget Hollywood: These Bloodthirsty Beauties Are for Real," *Smithsonian,* December 1992, p. 52.
4. D'Amato, p. 154 .
5. Natalie Angier, "Plants That Are Predators," *New York Times,* September 14, 2015, p. D1.
6. D'Amato, p. 29.
7. Mollie Rilstone, "Byblis Glandular Mucus," International Carnivorous Society, May 16, 2009, http://icps.proboards.com/thread/2929/byblis-glandular-mucus.

Chapter 3. Pits of Death

1. *Plants Behaving Badly*, directed by Steve Nicholls (Vienna, Austria: Terra Factual Studios, 2013), documentary.
2. "Carnivorous Plants/Insectivorous Plants," Botanical Society of America, accessed April 30, 2018, https://botany.org/Carnivorous_Plants/.

3. Donald E. Schnell, *Carnivorous Plants of the United States and Canada,* 2nd edition (Portland, Oreg.: Timber Press, 2002), p. 28.
4. Barry Rice, "Frequently Asked Questions, " International Carnivorous Plant Society, revised February 2012, http://www.sarracenia.com/faq/faq5538.html.
5. Peter D'Amato, *The Savage Garden* (Berkeley, Calif.: Ten Speed Press), p. 142.
6. *Plants Behaving Badly.*
7. C. M. Clarke, et al, "Tree Shrew Lavatories: A Novel Nitrogen Sequestration Strategy in a Tropical Plant," *Biology Letters* 5, no. 5 (October 2009), pp. 632–635.

Chapter 4. Active Trigger Traps

1. *Plants Behaving Badly*, directed by Steve Nicholls (Vienna, Austria: Terra Factual Studios, 2013), documentary.
2. Rainer Hedrich, "Carnivorous Plants," *Current Biology* 25, no. 3 (February 2, 2015), p. R99.
3. Ibid.
4. Donald E. Schnell, *Carnivorous Plants of the United States and Canada,* 2nd edition (Portland, Oreg.: Timber Press, 2002), p. 30.
5. Barry Rice, "Frequently Asked Questions," International Carnivorous Plant Society, revised June 2009, http://www.sarracenia.com/faq/faq5580.html.
6. "Carnivorous Plants/Insectivorous Plants," Botanical Society of America, accessed April 30, 2018, https://botany.org/Carnivorous_Plants/.

Chapter 5. Carnivorous Plants' Survival Manual

1. Axel Mithofer, "Carnivorous Pitcher Plants: Insight into an Old Topic," *Phytochemistry* 72, no. 13 (September 2011), pp. 1678–1682.
2. "Carnivorous Plants/Insectivorous Plants," Botanical Society of America, accessed April 30, 2018, https://botany.org/Carnivorous_Plants/.
3. Michael Lipski, "Forget Hollywood: These Bloodthirsty Beauties Are for Real," *Smithsonian,* December 1992, p. 52.
4. David E. Jennings and Jason R. Rohr, "A Review of Conservation Threats to Carnivorous Plants," *Biological Conservation* 144, no. 5 (May 2011), pp. 1356–1363.
5. Christopher Mele, "Venus Flytraps Need Protection from Poachers in North Carolina," *New York Times,* November 29, 2016, p. D2.

Glossary

antibiotic A substance that kills bacteria or prevents their growth.

aphid A tiny insect that feeds on plant sap.

bog Soggy, waterlogged ground that is high in acid and low in nutrients.

botanist A scientist who studies plants.

enzyme A protein that performs or speeds up chemical reactions.

fungus An organism that shares characteristics with plants, but is classified in a different kingdom. Fungi include mushrooms, yeast, mold, and toadstools.

gland A small organ that produces a substance used by the plant or animal.

habitat The natural home in which a plant or animal can thrive.

invertebrate An animal without a backbone.

larva The immature form of an insect.

lobe A rounded division or section of a larger plant or body part.

mucilage A sticky, gummy liquid produced by plants.

narcotic A drug that affects the normal function of a living thing.

rhizome An underground or underwater plant stem from which the roots and shoots of certain plants arise.

rotatorium A microscopic, three-sectioned roundworm.

terrestrial Based on land.

vulnerable At risk.

Further Reading

Books

Blevins, Wiley. *Ninja Plants: Survival and Adaptation in the Plant World.* Minneapolis, MN: Twenty-First Century Books, 2017.

Hewitt-Cooper, Nigel. *Carnivorous Plants: Gardening with Extraordinary Botanicals.* Portland, OR: Timber Press, 2016.

Kaelin, Matthew M. *The Sinister Beauty of Carnivorous Plants.* Atglen, PA: Schiffer Publishing, 2016.

Lawler, Janet. *Scary Plants!* New York, NY: Penguin Young Readers, 2017.

Websites

Botanical Society of America
botany.org/Carnivorous_Plants
Learn more about many species of carnivorous plants.

Hewlett-Cooper Carnivorous Plants
www.Hccarnivorousplants.co.uk
Explore more information about meat-eating plants and how to grow them.

International Carnivorous Plant Society
www.carnivorousplants.org
Dive deeper with articles, FAQs, and photos of carnivorous plants.

Index

A

Arthrobotrys obligiospora, 11

B

bladderworts, 8, 9, 31–34, 38
butterworts, 14–16, 23
Byblis, 20

C

Capsella bursa-pastoris, 11
carnivorous plants
    animals with immunities to, 38–39
    criteria for, 9
    food, 10–11
    growing at home, 40
    how their traps developed, 36–38
    human threat to, 39–41
    types of, 11–13
Carnivorous Plant Society, 9
caspid, 38
cobra lily, 21, 222

D

Darwin, Charles, 9–10, 28–29

F

flypaper plants, 14–20, 23, 28, 38

L

Liche, Carle, 5
Linneaus, Carolus, 7

M

Molinia caerulea, 11
mucilage, 18, 19

N

Nepenthes, 27

P

pitcher plants, 8, 9, 21, 22–27, 28, 38

R

rhizome, 23

S

Sarracenia flava, 24
sundews, 16–19

T

trigger trap plants, 28–34

V

Venus flytrap, 7, 28–34, 38, 40

Z

Zoophagus insidians, 11